HOUSE OF LORE

I Am A Bee

REBECCA AND JAMES MCDONALD

My colony lives in a hive that is made of wax and special bee glue called propolis. Our hive is our house. Sometimes we like to build hives in trees, fallen logs, caves, or even between rocks.

In a colony, every bee has a job to do. First, there's the queen bee. Her job is to make eggs. Next, are the drone bees. Their job is to help the queen make eggs. Last, but not least, are the worker bees. That's what I am, and we have a whole bunch of jobs to do!

As a young bee, my first jobs were to keep the hive clean and feed and take care of the colony. Luckily, worker bees are really good at working together and helping each other.

As I grew, so did my jobs. Once my body was able to make wax, I became a builder. I made sure there were enough rooms for all of the baby bees, and extra space to store lots of pollen, and nectar that would be made into honey.

By flapping our wings or vibrating our bodies, worker bees keep the hive at a perfect temperature, not too hot and not too cold, so wax can be shaped, glue can be spread, and honey can be made.

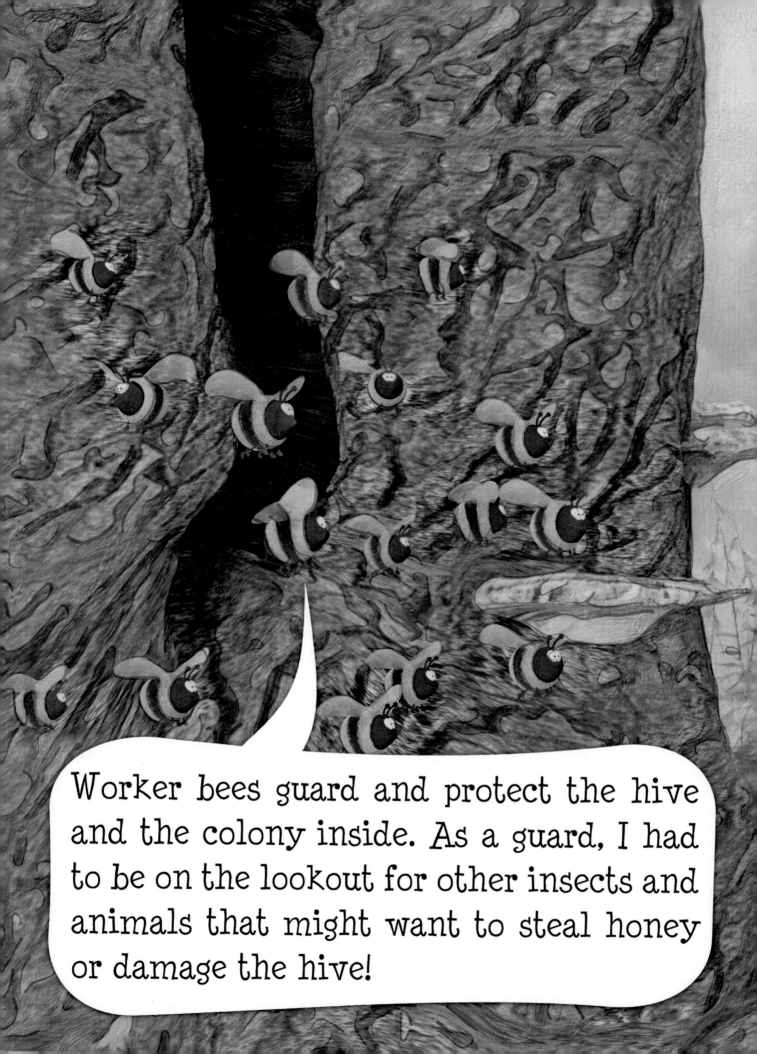

Worker bees guard and protect the hive and the colony inside. As a guard, I had to be on the lookout for other insects and animals that might want to steal honey or damage the hive!

Now that I'm an older bee, I have a new job. I'm a forager! Bees usually never leave the hive, unless there's an emergency, or if they're foraging to find food and water.

Being a forager is a really important job. I fly away looking for patches of blooming flowers that have lots of delicious pollen and sweet nectar. Nectar is a sugary juice, and pollen is a yellow dust. They're both my favorite foods.

I crawl inside a flower and load up as much as I can carry. I have a special pouch in my stomach for carrying nectar, and I have pollen baskets on both of my back legs for when I'm carrying extra pollen.

Pollen is really sticky, and I always end up covered in it. That makes plants happy, because when I fly to the next flower, I drop pollen, which helps plants make seeds. Scientists call this pollination. Lots of seeds mean more vegetables, fruits and pretty flowers for everyone!

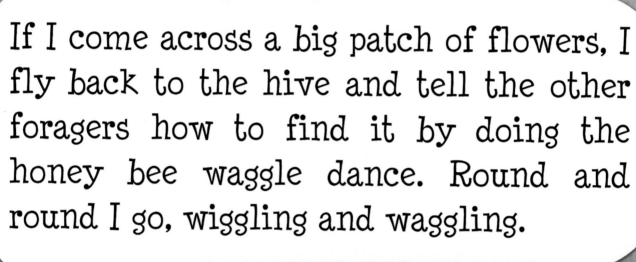

If I come across a big patch of flowers, I fly back to the hive and tell the other foragers how to find it by doing the honey bee waggle dance. Round and round I go, wiggling and waggling.

Storing lots of honey for winter is really important. When it's cold, honey bees stay inside the hive, eating the stored honey and flying close together in a big tight circle to keep warm.

Foragers fly all over the place. Sometimes that can cause us big problems. When we fly into places where people have sprayed chemicals to get rid of other bugs, it makes us get sick too. Chemicals can also drift into our hive, making it an unhealthy place to live.

People can help bees by not using chemicals that make bees sick. You can help by sharing what you've learned about honey bees with family, friends, and in your classroom.

What do honey bees live inside of?

What do honey bees like to eat?

How do forager bees tell each other where to find flowers?

How do bees help people?

How can people help bees?

I Am a Bee

Copyright © 2019 by Rebecca and James McDonald

ISBN: 978-1-950553-16-7
First House of Lore paperback edition, 2019
Visit us at www.HouseOfLore.net